Yesterdays and Imagining Realities
An Anthology of South African Poetry

Yesterdays and Imagining Realities
An Anthology of South African Poetry

First published in Tshwane, South Africa,
by impepho press in 2020
impephopress.co.za

ISBN 978-1-990998-78-2

Original poems edited by vangile gantsho, Tshifhiwa Given,
Mukwevho, Dominant Napoleon Munzhelele, Kwazi
Ndlangisa, Mbongeni Nomkonwana, Nakanjani G. Sibiya,
Sabelo Soko, Toni Giselle Stuart and Pieter Odendaal.
Cover by Banele Khoza
Book production by impepho press

This book is the initiative of the French Institute of South Africa in
partnership with Total South Africa and impepho press.

All illustrations appearing in this book were commissioned by the
French Institute of South Africa in partnership with Total South Africa.

Inside pages printed on 90 gsm Print Speed Cartridge paper (ECF pulp, certified 4 stars in the Green Star SystemTM, FSC® and EU Ecolabel). Cover printed on 300 gsm GalerieArt Plus Gloss (PEFC™; FSC®; EMAS; ISO 9001; ISO 14001; ISO 50001; ECF; FSC® C.o.C; PEFC™ C.o.C; OHSAS 18001; PEFC™ credit material; FSC® Mix; Toy Safety; Paper Profile; Archive Friendly). Outside cover is matt laminated for surface protection and handling, treat as plastic waste.

Yesterdays and Imagining Realities
An Anthology of South African Poetry

Contents

Foreword

Yesterdays and Imagining Realities

From 19th century poets such as Victor Hugo to slam artists such as Grand Corps Malade, poetry has always had a very special place in French literature. As words come together and become magic, poetry can convey emotions with an unparalleled intensity, while also allowing us to reflect on our societies, to understand, to disagree.

Léopold Sédar Senghor once said, "Poetry must not perish. For what would then happen to the World's hope?" His words are more relevant than ever in this unprecedented crisis. They are at the core of *Yesterdays and Imagining Realities*, as we all have witnessed how artists have risen in this time of isolation.

This anthology resonates with Africa 2020, a pan-African cultural season taking place in France from December 2020 to June 2021, and an invitation to see the world from an African perspective. The voices included in *Yesterdays and Imagining Realities: An Anthology of South African Poetry* have been selected following an invitation for young poets to submit work in any of South Africa's official languages, as part of our support to plurilingualism. Almost 400 poems have been shared with us, all carefully read by our experienced judges. The final selection of poems and illustrations is one we think will live on for years to come.

This project would not have been possible without our partners. I wish to warmly thank Total South Africa for their continuous support to the arts. I would also like to thank impepho press, Poetry Africa, the judges and illustrators, and last but not least, all the poets who answered our call.

Aurélien Lechevallier,
Ambassador of France to South Africa and Lesotho

Judges reflections

vangile gantsho

The responsibility of judging submissions that will then comprise a book is not a responsibility I take lightly. As a poet myself, I know the weight of rejection. I know how difficult it is to sometimes pick yourself up and still force yourself to hold on to the belief that you have something to say, and it's worth hearing. That you are talented. And this is not a "never", it's a "not right now". So I begin this reflection by acknowledging all the poets who submitted the 384 poems we received. It takes courage to send your work to strangers and trust that they will treat it with fairness and kindness.

When selecting the thirty poems that would make up the anthology *Yesterdays and Imagining Realities: An Anthology of South African Poetry*, I was looking for a range of poems that would collectively make for an interesting book. I wanted poems that were well-written, first and always foremost, as well as poems that showed multiple interpretations of the theme: history and imagined realities. I wanted poetry that reflects our multilingualism and rich oral history of storytelling, as well as poetry that is delicate and deliberate about creative crafting. Poems that range across the national and the personal, across histories and across imaginings. Poems that aren't afraid to colour outside the lines. And I am proud to say, that's what we found.

The selection process was gruelling though, I won't lie. Reading and re-reading poems. Drawing up lists and cutting them down. Finding out that some of the poems you liked were disqualified because they had been previously published. And sometimes, seeing the potential in a poem but realising that it would require a lot of editing to get it to where it needs to be, and there are poems that are already there. Once we had individually selected our picks, we had to cross check our lists and come to a collective selection. It took an eight hour Zoom call of reading, translating, discussing sometimes disagreeing, to get to this book. But we did it.

It's no surprise that I was drawn to the more-women-centered poems, ("Loving like our mothers", "Incwadi Yokufa" and "Wolf Girl"). But I must say, I was also impressed by poems that were willing to explore other realities and live outside popular rhetoric. "A Book of Dead Black Boys", "Smartie Town", "met die sterre gepla", "Township South Africa", "Cloaked Words", and "When Words Fail". I was also moved by the poems that reminded me of why our indigenous languages are so beautiful. The poems that sang through the tears, particularly "Khotsi A Si Na Ndavha" and "Ikati ilel'eziko".

The most rewarding part of this process, I think, was finding out the names behind the poems. Realising there are so many amazing poets that we don't know, yet. And also realising that for some poets, we had chosen multiple submissions. The truth is, this country has so much talent. And the future of South African literature is in good hands.

Camagu.

Tshifhiwa Given Mukwevho

I read all the poems with keen interest and, while busy engaging the poems, it dawned on me that the young poets are endowed with the talents which we surely need to celebrate as a country. They do not only write from different cultural, social and economic backgrounds but varied artistic experimentations galore are in the poems they present us with. As judges we found ourselves spoilt for choice when it came to selecting poems for inclusion in the anthology. In some cases, we obviously agreed instantly on some poems where they had struck us all with their beauty, the use of figurative language, and the honesty with which the value is added to the poem, such as in "A Book of Dead Black Boys" by Xabiso Vili, "A Face of Many" by Mthabisi Sithole, "Die Palimpses" by Wade Smit, "Khotsi A Si Na Ndavha" by Ronewa Mukwevho, and "Incwadi yokufa" by Bongeka Nkosi.

While the majority of poems submitted exuded appealing literary excellence in many ways poetic, I was somehow disappointed at the fact that most of those poems were either not edited or proofread. It would seem like poets just submitted first drafts, without bothering about reading the lines out to detect any unwanted chaff. Just imagine having read six beautiful stanzas and in the seventh (which is the last stanza) you are confronted by a glaring grammatical error followed by another one.

Having said all that, I am pleased to say that I have enjoyed the judging or reading experience; I have been really enriched by the experience.

Nakanjani Sibiya

It was an honour and privilege indeed to be tasked with the exciting and enriching task of participating as one of the adjudicators for this competition. The response from poets who were invited to send their creative pieces was overwhelming, particularly considering the upheavals and emotional challenges that permeated the period during which the call for entries was made.

The daunting, albeit fulfilling exercise was that of perusing the three hundred odd poems and selecting the cream of the crop for shortlisting. It was quite heartwarming when the judges' individual selections matched. The bulk of the entries was captivating, to say the least, with many poets executing the creative flow of words with exceptional dexterity. Of course, there were disappointing exceptions with glaring weaknesses that reflected unacceptable disregard for competition rules and basic requirements for a well-written poem.

For me, what stood out was the wide variety of stylistic features that made each poet unique and true to the craft, as evident in "You are Here", by Sarah Lubala. Some chose the well-beaten route, marked by preoccupation with rigid form and somewhat contrived rhyme scheme, while others preferred big words at the expense of simple yet apt words that enhance appreciation of the message and ambience of the poem. There is an obvious need for workshops for some poets, particularly in showing that while poems are by definition meant for performance, form and stylistic elements should be perfected at composition level, for ease of publishing when such chances arise.

Undoubtedly, artists can sometimes be intimidated and inhibited by a specific theme around which they are expected to compose. Thematic distribution was quite revealing, particularly with regard to areas of interface in the poets' take on a plethora of challenges and the impact thereof on ordinary people. Some voices resonated and bemoaned the plight of the disenfranchised youth and women who have to contend with atrocities. There was also a longing to retrieve the lost past where Ubuntu and collective wisdom thrived. But, it was heart-warming to glean some positive outlook from the poets and a throbbing quest to tread ahead and enjoy life amidst the restrictive hurdles.

As expected, my interest was more inclined towards isiZulu. There is a tendency to focus more on performance techniques and style at the expense of how a poem looks on the paper in terms of overall arrangement. In some cases, it's only when the poet performs that one gets to be moved. This poses challenges when considering it for inclusion in published form, and necessitates line rearrangement. This can be true of "Emasisweni", for instance.

There is no doubt about the importance of this anthology. Not only will it enhance confidence and self-confidence for poets but it will unearth and showcase new talent across backgrounds. Its multilingual mix is also a refreshing feature and invaluable in showing that while poets emerge from different linguistic and cultural backgrounds, their artistic creations and expressions transcend borders and merge as one voice. The prominence of female poets in the anthology is also a very welcome feature.

Toni Giselle Stuart

I said yes to the request to judge this competition because the theme speaks directly to my work. As a poet, I have been exploring South African histories and herstories, to re-imagine and re-write them in a way that renders us fully human. So, I was excited about the chance to read and hear how young poets are approaching this field of writing.

When I sat down to read the 384 entries, I was overwhelmed. The sheer number was a lot to get through. It took me a day and a half to work through the list and read each poem. I pulled out the poems that spoke to me, and ended up with a list of 80. I re-read those 80 (often more than once) to get to my shortlist of 20 poems. There were lots of poems that spoke to the theme of history, while very few of the total entries that spoke to imagined realities. The poems that did, did so in interesting, and unusual ways.

I was particularly moved by the poems that intentionally used words in new, unusual and interesting ways, and in doing so, showed us different perspective on the very familiar themes and stories of our history, as a country. I was also drawn to the poems that successfully wove together personal and collective histories, and showed how they continue to influence and impact each other in the present.

Our judges meeting was scheduled for two hours. The plan was to each present our shortlist and then make our selection from there. The meeting lasted eight hours. Yes, an eight-hour Zoom call, because we were intentional and thorough and meticulous. Any poem that two or more judges had chosen in their shortlists, made it to our initial list of 30. Then we went through every single poem on each of our shortlists, and read them together, to decide if we should include it or not. We discussed and debated, the merits of one poem versus another.

vangile had a keen ear and eye for the overall feel of the anthology, which helped us arrive at more than just a final list of the best 30 poems. We wanted to create an intentional experience for the reader: a book that had range in language, poetry style and form, as well as theme. The process was gruelling but it was worth it.

Congratulations to every poet whose work has been included in this groundbreaking anthology. I hope you all keep writing and sharing your words with the world.

Apho igazi lenu lithe lathontsela khona,
Komila intyatyambo evumba limnandi,
Eliya kuthwalwa ngamaphiko empepho,
Zithi zonk'izizwe zilirogole.

JJR Jolobe

Untitled
Keneilwe Mokoena

Warped History

Tshifhiwa Itai Ratshiungo

somewhere in this warped history of a romantic struggle lies the truth
mother hears us sing *asina mali*
and remembers
  father returned a bruised man gleaming with hope
and remembers
  the struggle is not far from yesterday
and the policeman skin of her skin
  who commanded *"dompas"*
  and she did not rattle as he flipped through it
  and her suitcase murmuring *"Jehova's witness"*

while father dug diamonds for the man
held its worth in the palms which slapped music from his gumboots
mother carried around the good news in the watchtower

working men will never dishearten when they work
singing sombrely the dream of hope: *tomorrow morning*

while father broke rocks in prison
mother sent the children to school
she hurried the firstborns out of katlehong
she saw to it he escaped the borders
and kept the vinyl of the songs no one was afraid to remember

she toured the houses from street to street to vilakazi
evangelising "tomorrow morning" hidden in the watchtower
when the hopes of many dwindled when many died
when the hopes despaired when many were buried alive
a bloodbath of youths martyred before they could taste this rainbow

we strike tomorrow morning
we fight tomorrow morning
freedom is tomorrow morning
tomorrow morning becoming a story of soon

father stepped into power in the colours
of a bruised man gleaming with hope
he vowed land tomorrow morning
and so did his descendant
     and his descendant
     and his

the country is stolen in blood money
we her great and grandchildren beg men wearing freedom's colours
for land belonging to a people who suffered from nothing of their fault
we still cry the plight of their betrayal: *thina sizwe*
in freedom colours struggled into power

we forget the meaning of yesterday's sacrifice
we forget the struggle is not far from yesterday
wearing school uniform to taverns irreverently
commemorating the sacrifice of youths who died for learning
as youths today have died for learning

it is easier to forget when these stories are omitted and left to romantic
    imagination
/ these realities are silent from the mouths of men and women who
    bruised and gleamed
with hope toiling for this land / they do not want to remember what
    they can still see:

tomorrow morning is a story of soon.

Vhufa Hashu

Masindi Netshakhuma

Nandi naa iwe muḓuhulu wa Ṅwali
Naa u a tou livhala vhufa matsheloni mangafha?
Takuwa u ḽi dzwinge sheḓo
Sa tsiwana musanda yo lindela ḓuvha ḽa tsengo.

Naho vha tshi nga vha tshe vho ri vhofha vha vhuṱali
Zwa mulovha zwi ngelekanyoni
A ri livhali.
Kha dzi tshatshame tsindi sa malelega seli
Ni vale munango ya ḽa Afurika Tshipembe mikanoni
Uri vha fhire vha tshi tama na vhatsinda

Tevhela ngomalungundu he vha i kudza hone
U lidze dza vha hashu vha tshi bva ngei Congo
He vha awedza mihumbulo Mapungubwe
Ndi amba nga ṅwaha wa mmbo
Tsikidzi dzi sa athu vha hone
Ri sa athu pamba marukhu na dzirokho.

Ndi amba iwe mukololo wa Afurika Tshipembe
Iwe voḓa, dzuvha ḽa Vhembe
Iwe u no tamiwa nga mirafho na mirafho
Takuwa u tshine malende
U hake deu u tshine domba na vhaṅwe.

Miṱodzi yau ro i pfa nga ṅwaha uḽa
I tshi ri u wela fhasi ya lila sa ngoma
Ṋamusi a u tsha vha tshipondwa zhinda ḽa Afurika
Ndi ri takuwa u fare thonga u tshine tshifasi na tshikona
U si na ṱhoni sa Vhashona

Ndi amba na vhoiwe vhomakhadzi
Naa ni a tou phasa nga a u fhisa
Zwisima zwo ḓadza thavha?

Kha vhonale maredo
Nkho dzi tshi bva zwisimani

Aa Makhotsimunene
I shavha i sia muinga i tshi ya fhi?
Godani ndila i tswuke ni livhe ha Tshikamuroho
Minwaha ya fumi fhedzi zwi nga ro vuwa ro livhala sialala na mvelele
Naa no tou lindela u miliwa nga vhadali naa?

Ndi' takuwa nwana wa Muvenda
U divhudze u fa na u tshila
U tshi fela vhufa hashu sa tshileli musanda
Takuwani vhaduhulu vha ha Tshikamuroho
Ni kande ho kandaho vhomakhulukuku
Sialala na mvelele ni zwi pute
Sa lupfumo lwa u vhinga dzuvha la Afurika.

Our Heritage (Vhufa Hashu)

Tr. Domina Napoleon Munzhelele

Hey you, the grandchild of Ṅwali!
Do you overlook our heritage so early?
Position yourself for sheḓo,
Wearing it like a man in verdict of the Chief's kraal

Though the brewing of the new wisdom emerges
Our past is rooted in our minds – we forget not
Let all the men everywhere wear tsindi
Populating it in all the borders of South Africa
So that even foreigners will envy its beauty.

Let Vhavenḓa revive the sacred Ngomalungundu drum
Reviving the songs which they sung on their way from Congo
Migrating until they took rest at Mapungubwe
I mean during the bygone years of living
When our culture was European blank.

Hey you, the princess of South Africa
You, the daughter, the rose of Limpopo
You are imitated by generations and generations
Stand up and perform malende dance
Form a circle and perform domba dance

I remember you shedding tears
Your tears were falling down like rain
Nowadays your prince's face is crying no more
Rise and hold your stick doing tshikona dance
Be proud as Shona people.

I challenge you, the royal princesses,
How do you conduct your ritual of worship?
Do you sprinkle the hot water in ritual?
Springs are galore in the mountains,

Let us see the multi-coloured stripped cloths
Of Venḓa women carrying clay water pots from the springs.

I challenge you, the princes,
Why do you abandon your home?
Pack your luggage and return home
All ten years, we have forgotten our culture and tradition

Stand up Venḓa child
Tell yourself it is do or die
Die for your heritage as the royal heirs and heroines
Stand up all the grandchildren of Venḓas
Follow the footsteps of grandfathers
Preserving our culture and tradition
Preserving it like the married princess of Africa.

Iimbali ZikaNongcinga

Anathi Jonase

Aaa! Zwe likaPhalo, Aaa! Zwe likaRharhabe,
Khanizole mawethu ndingqishe, ndibharhamle ndithethe ngeembali
  zikaNongcinga,
Khanizole kaloku ndigqogqe, ndiqhuqha ndithethe ngenzala
  kaNongcinga,
Ndiboleken' iindlebe ndigqume, ndityatyadule ndithethe ngempumelelo
  yeembali zikaNongcinga.
Ndeb' endal' eyayi bumb' usapho ngengubo yothando nemanvano,
Ndeb' endal' eyayi qokelel' usapho eziko ilunik' imfudumalo
  nomanyano,
Diza dal' owaye ncumis' iintsana maxa wamb' ezoyikisa,
Nto yayi qoqosh' iqhuqh' isimilo semveku iselula,
Nto yayi ngqimbilil' inambitheka bubumnandi besithethe.
Ncas' ephalazwa yincindi yosiba kwi zidwash' ezimhlophe kuvel'
  ukukhanya,
Ncas' eqanjwa kwaNongcinga ngeenjongo zokuphilisa nokumbumb'
  umntu,
Wen' usakhile isizwe waqeqesha nabantu baso,
Wena waphila ngexesha la mandulo usaphila kwanamhlanje.

Xa kunamhlanje sikubukela kumabona-kude sibuye nomphako
  wengomso,
Xa kunamhlanje utyhutyha kumaziko wezemfundo uqulath' impiliso
Apha kuwe, kuphuma iincutshe neencutshekazi zababhali,
Kumakhasi wezo nxebelelwano sigqub' emswaneni wakho nto
  kaNongcinga
iSizwe sinyathel' umzila weenyawo zakho nto ndini,
Aaa! Mbali zikaNongcinga, Aaa! Zwe le mfundiso.

The History of Nongcinga (Iimbali ZikaNongcinga)

Tr. Mbongeni Nomkonwana

Aaa! Nation of Phalo, Aaa! Nation of Rharhabe
Grant me the silence to gloat and boastfully narrate the histories of
    Nongcinga,
Grant me and my bag of stories the silence to speak of Nongcinga's
    descendants,
Lend me your ears and allow me to bellow the history of Nongcinga's
    success.
You draped your family with a warm, harmonious blanket of love,
You became a fireplace of benevolent warmth and symphony,
The nurturer who made children giggle and cry,
Guardian who carved respect and discipline out of young ones,
You were a rich, palatable, history of our culture and customs.
You danced on white pages to cite and summon light,
The wise one whose calling is the flowering of humanity,
You have built this nation and moulded its people,
You have lived and stood the test time.

Today we watch you on television and take food for thought, from your
    basket of wisdom,
Today, institutions of learning can spell your name,
You birth proficient, profound wordsmiths of all kinds,
On social media, we bow to your name,
Our nation continues to follow the path of your gigantic footsteps,
Aaaa! History of Nongcinga, Aaa! Well of enlightenment.

Emasisweni

Cebolenkosi Nkosi

Ngeze ngageq' amagula ngowakith' umlando, kepha
Ngivumeleni ngikhulume ngiphos' itsh' esivivaneni.
Zul' omnyama kaMalandela ondlela zimhlophe, Nkayishane
kaMenzi eyaphuz' umlaza ngameva. Soze salibal' amav' ebutho
lika Zulu omnyam' asal' empini yaseSandlwane. Ngingakhohlwa kanjani
amaqhaw' abhejis' umfula wabomvu kweyase Ncome. Ngivumeleni
ke nami kowakith' umlando ngincom' okuhle kodwa ngawo. Lelo gaz'
elachitheka soze salikhohlwa, angithi nasikhipha nasikhulul' ebugqileni
bamaqadasi. Ngenxa yobuqhawe benu mina ke ngithi azibuyel'
emasisweni. Nithi benazi ukuthi enakulwela kuleli zwe sekwaphenduka
ize leze. Nithi benazi ukuthi umhlaba sewasiphendukela njengotshwal'
esiswini.

Ngeze ngageqa amagula ngowakithi umlando, kepha ngicela
Ningivumeleni ngithungel' injobo enhl' ebandla. Kodadengendlala
 bamasimu
Enasishiyela bona sekwalala is'khotha. Ezanamhlanje izizukwalane
 azisakushay'
indiva konke lokho. Phezu komkhono lethwes' ihlobo.
Phela bekubhukulwa kulinywe ngenhloso yokuxosh' ikati eziko.
Yek' intomb' isashelwa emfuleni iminyakanyaka kugug' iscathulo
 emabhungwini. Angisay'phathi ke eyomgcagco esigcawini kusinwa
kudedelwane ibutho nekhetho. Ziwushaye maqede kuchithwe iviyo
 ezinsizweni
lidlale umgagela odongeni. Ngeke ngisaliphatha elokuqonywa
 kwamabhungu
kumiswe iduku. Konke lokho sekwaba umlando njengokulala
 kwamaqhawe akithi,
kwaphela sengathi akukaze kwaba khona kuhle kwamazolo kuqhamuk'
 ilanga.
Vukani nibe idloz' elihle maqhawe akithi sibuyele kowakithi umlando.

Yize ngiseyiqhumisamponjwana ng'yafung' emandulo kwakumnandi.
Yize ukhakhayi lwami lusemanzi kepha ngamehlo engqondo ng'yabona.

Kwaphelelaphi ukusiswa kwemfuyo kuleyo mndeni edl' imbuya ngothi.
Yeka kusakhethwa amandikane kusengwa, kudliwa amas' egula.
Namhlanje noma begula baphuthum' izibhedlela kunamakhamb' esintu.
Kwankomo kamama isishabalele izingane zanamhlanje ziphisana ngayo
Kungakhokhiwe. Azibuy' emasisweni ngoba laph' ezikhona
    zingumhlambi
Kazelusile. Kusile, ayisuke yonk' inkungu ekhungath' esakith' isizwe.
Nami ngale nkondlo ngicela ningizwe, sizw' esinsundu bamban'
    okwakini
Nikuqinise. Ngithe ngeze ngageqa amagula kepha ngithi azibuyel'
    emasisweni

Back to Basics (Emasisweni)

Tr. Sabelo Soko

I cannot tell you everything in our history
But please allow me to throw this in
Black Zulu of Malandela with bright trails
Nkayishana of Menzi who drank constellations through the thorns
We cannot forget the efforts of black Zulu warriors
Who lost their lives in Sandlwane
How can I forget the heroes who turned Ncome red with blood
Allow me, in our history, to compliment the best
The blood that was shed will never be forgotten
It released us from the vile grip of oppression
For your heroic sake
I say, we should go back to basics
For what you have fought for has become naught
The world has turned against us as does its heavy spirits

I really cannot tell you everything in our history
But let me make this public
Over the rampant hunger
The generation of today feasts on ignorance
The hectors of land left for us have become wild fields
In the olden days when Spring approached
We rolled up our sleeves and went to work
For work kept our homes and guts warm
When young men courted women for years by the river
Until the soles of their shoes wore off
Between the stick fights and warrior chants
There echoed the joy of a raised scarf
The beads and the wedding dance
All have become *history*, like the death of our heroes
Gone as if they were never here
Gone like morning dew after sunrise
Awake and become good ancestors you mighty heroes
Let us go back to a history that is our own

The top of my head might still be soggy, but my imaginary eyes are
    sharp
I might still be growing, but I know, there was bliss in the past
What happened to the livestock that was kept to support the deprived
In those days of abundant milk
When the nation feasted on the cream overflowing from a calabash
Today the sick rush to hospitals neglecting their indigenous roots
Donating their mother's cow before negotiations are concluded
We need to go back to basics,
For this here, is no man's land
With the new dawn upon us, may the mist that covers our nation
    dissipate
With these words I plead with you nation with bright pathways
Hold what is your own, hold it fast

I did say, I cannot tell you everything
We just really need to go back to basics.

You Change

Nqobile Lombo

It is so interesting to me
what you see
and how that changes

You sit, and hear of Dannhauser
your grandmothers worked there as labourers
one escaped to Durban
the others followed
This is land they worked on

You are in Hammarsdale, Mpumalanga township
you are in a four bedroom house
you are inherently hearing of the land you lost

So you look at your hands
what you see
and how that changes

You listen to your Grandfather
who was forcibly removed from Cato Manor
in the 1950s and put into makeshift camps
with strangers
with children

So you look at yourself
what you see
and it changes

You document how a mother burns herself to death
after she could not provide for her children
when the act – THAT act – forcibly removed them
and here her children are
on the land they claimed

So you look to God
because you are changing

Then you read
you read that most churches still own the land
inherited by colonial rulers
and they refuse to let it go

Then you don't see yourself anymore

Ikat'ilel'eziko

Mbasa Setsana

Huntshu Mzantsi Afrika Huntshu!
Huntshu Bahlali Huntshu!
Vumani le mvumo ithelekisa oosathana
Nimdanise umthyoli
Iintshaba zilangazelele impumelelo yethu.

Vukani bantwana boMzantsi Afrika Vukani!
Inyathi ibuzwa kwabaphambili
Hloniphani ooyihlo nihloniphe noonyoko
Mamelani amazwi abo ukuze ningadideki
Nidilizeke nidalelwe amashwa obomi.

Okhokho bayiphefumlela le kululeko yethu
Thina Bantu bantsundu nengxenye yabamhlophe
Salwa ukuze sikhululeke, siphile, siqaqambe
Sihambe uhambo lodandatheko noluphucukileyo.

Yintoni lutsha lakokwethu, lento nineempixano nabazali!
Nixhaphaza abadlezana, abantu ababenibeleka emiqolo
Iinyembezi zoonozala ziphalala umhla nezolo
Iintliziyo zabo zilijaja ligazi
Iintombi azisapheki zithinjwe yintombi kaludiza
Abazali bona bayalila.

Thabathani inxaxheba emfundweni, ngoba sesona sixhobo
    esakukhulula isizwe sethu.

Ewe John nawe Linda
Wena Dingalethu nawe Pravashni
Dingalethu and Pravashni
Masiguqule isimo sentlalo yethu
Singadlwengulwa yinkxwaleko

Gqobo gqushum gqwa!
Khala sithonga sesizwe
Iingqondo ziyaqhekeka ziqhathwa
Ziqhelwa ngamaqhinga
ooqhoqhoqho bayaphela
Ngenxa yeziyobisi zoosathana.
Iingaba zizenzo zentlupheko ezo?
Ndithi hayi kuni, hayini kuni ninonke!

From Grahamstown to Cape Town
Mdantsane and Soweto
Ikamva masilibange lelethu
Nokuba ikati ingalal'eziko
Imfundo yona mayibekho.

Izihange, ootsotsi
Izigebenga izigilamkhuba.
Mazikhuthazwe luluntu, zithabathe uxanduva.

Uhambo lweminyaka lwakhulula esi sizwe
Zatsho iingqondo zaqokelelana, zaqiqa, zaqina.
Sadloba, sadlamka, sadlisela, kwamnandi, saqaqamba.

Ubomi sisipho, impilo iyasetyenzelwa.

Ndithi ntlupheko hlupheka awusoze usidilize
Abo balibalekayo basayidlala inxaxheba ebomini bethu
Sizizikhakhamela ezifuze uMadiba.
Aaaaaa! Dalibhunga....

The cat slumbers by the fire place (Ikat'ilel'eziko)

Tr. Mbongeni Nomkonwana

All hail South Africa!
All hail the people of South Africa!
Chant such that the devils become disgruntled
Evil must not rejoice in our suffering
Enemies shall marvel at our success.

Open your eyes children of South Africa the sun has risen
Seek wisdom from the elders
Honour the community that birthed you
Listen to reason and embody their teachings
Do not become drudge to the misfortunes of this world.

Our forebears fought for liberation.
Dark or light they stood side by side
To fight for freedom, breath, and prosperity
We embarked on a journey of misery and enlightenment.

The youth dims the light of their torchbearers
Prey on the ones whose backs bear the scars of our upbringing
Our mothers' tears perish on this earth daily
Their hearts heavy with blood
And as little girls trade kitchens with dance floors
Our parents' cries become prayers.

Take pride in educating yourselves for you shall one day liberate this
    nation.

To John and Linda
Dingalethu and Pravashni
Stay awake
Before misery visits your bedside to molest you

Bullet…Shit…Bang!
Sound the nation's gunshots

Our minds manifest fragmented thoughts
From all these lies and fabricated truths
Throats are drying up
We are thirsty for more of the devil's poison
Has poverty become our distorted reality?
Not anymore, enough is enough.

From Grahamstown to Cape Town
Mdantsane and Soweto
Claim the future as yours
While poverty seems to be the being of our beings
We must be in constant pursuit of knowledge.

Criminals, street thugs,
Murders and thieves,
Must be inspired to become champions of change

The "Long Walk to Freedom" emancipated this nation
Freed our minds and illuminated our thoughts
We rejoiced, played, showed off, celebrated, basked.

Life is a gift, but living is a choice.

I say poverty must suffer in silence.
The forgotten ones are teaching us resilience.
We are royals to who take after the great Madiba.

Aaaaaa! Dalibhunga....

Facelessness
Mxolisi Dolla Sapeta

Township South Africa

Ntseka Masoabi

Imagine the *so-called* township
South Africans living in paved
and well maintained
gardens with large swimming pools.

Imagine Sipho and Nombaza doing their late-night
prayers without the gigantic Alexandra rats
hearing their prayers.
Or, Dieketseng,
in her tin-and-brick shack,
still doing her mathematics assignment despite her
mother's lazy moans from her
drunk lover's thrusts.

Imagine Dimakatso being heard
not from the way she mis-pronounces difficult English words,
but from her pure genius.

Imagine,
imagine the townships filled to the brim with happy
so-called black South Africans
who are not resisting,
nor wailing,
but genuinely
happy.

Smartie Town

Keith Lewis

ses-en-twintig
is die lewensverwagting van die laaities hier in die wild west
agt-en-twintig as hy sy kaarte reg dowwel
fraternities van heuninggeel babas is gewapen met messegoed
wat die ou girl nog afbetaal by huisvriend
hulle klein voetjies beman verlepte territory soos tjoekieheining
die general sit in sy smartie box vêr van die slagpale
bevele surf op speeksel uit sy goue put
'n sel voëltjies fluit
guy fawkes ry op 'n vaalperd deur die brandmaer strate
die polisie is rolbossies
maandag blou babas kruip terug crib toe in 'n kis
lyke wat lyk soos ek pose in hulle matriekafskeid suits
smartie town is 'n spaza shop vir groen grafte

Smartie Town (tr.)

Tr. Pieter Odendaal

twenty-six
is the life expectancy of laaities here in the wild west
twenty-eight if you play your cards well
fraternities of honey yellow babies are armed with knives
that the old gal is still settling with a family friend
their small feet garrison wilted territory like jail fences
the general sits in his smartie box far away from the abattoir
orders surf on spit from his gilded well
caged birds whistle
guy fawkes gallops through rawboned streets on a pale horse
the police are tumbleweeds
on monday blue babies crawl back to crib in a coffin
bodies like mine pose in their prom suits
smartie town is a spaza shop for fresh graves

A Portrait of my Father in the Afterlife

After Safia Elhillo

Busisiwe Mahlangu

My father's face taught me how to see danger unfold   eyes hold a fire
first   raging out of control. The nose feels uncomfortable warmth   it
burns the skin meeting at its sides.   The cheeks dry out.   The forehead
folding rankled.   The mouth open, speaking & smiling.   His mouth is
the last location of danger   this is the destination   this is where he
will arrive to break himself & cut into us with the pieces.   The lips
shake & let out a small sound.   This is the part you   run.
My father taught me how to see danger when it runs toward me.   I
should've seen this man transforming to inferno   but the fire was so
small, it kept me warm   & kept me meeting at his sides to protect him.
I am sorry baba   I did not see his anger explode.   Just as i did not see
you that time you flushed the father's day card down the toilet   because
it was not a pack of cigarettes
You told me to focus, baba   You did not tell me to fight   You gave me
a class on men whose anger is bigger than their bodies.   Their hunger for
ribs, for ankles, for ears, for fresh skin, cannot be fed a sorry. I will stop
apologising to sad men.

A book of dead black boys

Xabiso Vili

Anthology, which means a book of poems, is Greek for flowers

The black boy, he lies in a flowerbed
and wild chrysanthemums bloom from his eyes.
Wilting garlands and thorns adorn his head,
his floating tongue sheds petals as he dies.

This dark child wore a sparkling daisy crown,
cried when he found himself soft.
Incandescence, like us, are prone to drown -
watch how we spill cracked concrete when we cough.

This world would bury a flower's lament,
have the audacity to call them seeds.
His breath was gut-filled with soil and cement,
white knuckle plucked because you thought him weeds.

This thirsty earth must be fertile by now,
enough coffins to prepare your soil.
But when the black grows after the plough,
will you still use those hands for sweat and toil?

How I envy the lonely wand'ring cloud,
I write only of trees, and wreaths, and shroud.

Khotsi A Si Na Ndavha

Ronewa Mukwevho

Zwifhondo zwi khou tou ditshelela ndodo
Vhone tshavho ndi u sokou longondo na gondo
Feḓa ḽavho ḽo swika na Lwamondo
Ngeno vhana vha tshi ṋanzwa banga vha lala
Vhone tshavho hu u omba gologodo
Ndo tou pfa nga luṱhweṱhwe lu tshi vha remela phele muratho
Ngeno mafhondo avho vha tshi tou a sumba vha tshi fhira nga gondo
Vho vha vho ri ri ḓo funana u swika ḽa tswime ḽi tshi tota tombo
Ngavhe ḽiṅwe ḓuvha vha tshi welwa nga khombo
Vha u ṱavhe mukosi wa nḓala u no ongolela sa mbudzi ya ngei
    Madimbo

Ngoho vha penya khole vha si musuku, vha tshi tswima dombo
Vho ṱuwa vha tshi' vha yo rema basha ngei thavhani
Nga ngoho vho ḽi dzhena ḓaka nga ṱhoho
Na zwino vha ṱoḓi vha tshee ngeyo
Mutsinda ndi khwiṋe shaka ndi bulayo
Ngoho ndo tenda uri ndi tshidzimba tsha a si na maṋo
Ndi tama vha zwi ḓivhe uri kholomo ya nḓila a i fhedzi hatsi
Na dzi no ya mathaga danga dzi a ḽi ḓivha
I tou vha mukandangalwo lufu lu milenzheni
Tshivhi tshavho vha dzula vho tshi kungela khunduni
Tshi tou vha tshinembenembe khambana ya Funzani
Dzunde ḽavho ḽi songo tou vha luvhandaladzi lu fhedzaho marevho ḽo
    ṱanama
Ndi ngoho ḽinoni fulu a ḽi vhulahwi, ḽi na malumbulela
Ya tou vha nyavhumbwa wa dagaila vha kanda vho vha vhumbaho
Ndi tama vha zwi ḓivhe uri muthu a si tshiṱangadzime
Hu ḓi nga munwe muthihi a u ṱusi mathuthu

Nyamuvhuya ha shayi thando, a sa vha mbava ndi muloi
Fhedzi vha zwi ḓivhe uri maano a vhambwa nga luvhadzi
Vha tou vha ḽa Makahane nga u vha vhambisa vhathu mikumba nga
    maṋo

Vha lingedza u khukhuna luombeni, thunda nnḓa i ya vhonala
Yo vha i tshi shavha muinga i tshi ya fhi
Fhedzi hu ḓi naka nthuleni, nkhwesini i a vhavha
Vha zwi ḓivhe uri tshe wa da iwe tshilavhi na murundo wa phofu u ḓo
    vhuya wa ṅwa
Ri ḓo vhona ro lala, u vuwa ri tshi shavha u lenga
Ri ḓo vhona hune ha ḓo fhelela phuna na ṋotshi.
Ndaa!!

A Careless Father (Khotsi A Si Na Ndavha)

Tr. Domina Napoleon Munzhelele

Your children are fending for themselves on their own,
But you wander around and around aimlessly.
Your stench reeks from far and beyond
But your children starve day and night
Yours is to smoke marijuana
I heard about your whereabouts through the grapevine
You only point at your children as you pass by
You vowed to love me for infinity
I wish one day you are plunged into troubles
Overcome with the tears of peeling onions

Though you glitter like gold, you are a burning stone

You used to go out like you were coming back
But you went out for good and never returned
We still wait for you
It is true, sometimes strangers are more important than relatives
Even cattle go to graze and return
They know the kraal in which they belong
Remember, when you walk wherever you go
Death accompanies your life wherever you go
Your sin is your handbag, a part of your life
It is a necklace around your neck
Pray that you do not join the soil too soon
I swear, you will not die before you pay
You have forgotten all that I helped you with
Remember that a human being is not an island
You cannot stand or sail alone
One man cannot beat a team

I realised that flowers hide stinging bees
    So they say; once bitten twice shy
You are like a king in the land of cruel monsters
Who does things secretly and is ashamed in the light

You are the heavy bearer of the burden
He does not want to carry
One day is one day, when you will pay for your deeds
We will sit back and do nothing, waiting for your cursed day
We will just wait patiently, waiting for your day of reckoning.

A Metaphor for Africa

Zizipho Bam

I know what it feels like to be empty,
I have felt the gruesome stare of insufficiency.
It has burrowed holes deep enough
to accept this nothingness
you have claimed for me.

I know the cracking voice of poverty.
I can tell the rising inflictions of pity in your questions.

I do not need a breakdown of my short falls,
I have collapsed enough empires to know
how far up my spine stretches,
how low into the soil my roots dig,
and how many borders my blood has crossed
only to spill on the other side of the river.

I have not come for that.
There is a song of courage
at the bottom of my belly
humming itself into a thunderstorm.
I am a natural disaster of rage rumbling within.

My mind is a nimbus cloud
of reasons to exhale your patronising charity.

I have drowned in the Nile of my tears
each time you called me third world greedy.
Each time you beat your drums,
my arid heels cracked open.
The muscles of my Victoria snapped and tore.
Brittle and old have become my bones.

You have drunk me empty.

You have preached false hope to my people.
Your kind of Judas, sold me nothing
but dreams with starving children on postcards.

You have romanticised my ruggedness,
called my pigment primitive
and lured my people into your machine.

You cannot erase the smell of incense
from our memory.
My courage is a boiling pot of herbs
to cure the vanity, you have drilled in me.

I am washing away the shame you felt for me.
I have come to gather the last of my unwritten suffering.

I have come to collect the remains of my people,
the stories you have tried to tell on my behalf
and the songs I have sung to teach you my tongue.
From now on, clap it out if you still cannot pronounce my clan names.

But do not call our fathers, "The man in the green blanket".
My tongue weighs the entire ocean in my mouth,
my tongue is a wave.

Every time I want to speak
The Tina River of my Xhosa is washed out
by the Pacific Ocean English I have been taught to swim in.
I am drowning.
There is no Zulu, Sotho or Pedi word for "life jacket".

I have no name here.
You twist my ancestors inside out and turn them into cloaks of burden
    for my shoulders.

I have grown sores on the mountains of my back because of this war
    with myself.
My heart is a shattered dime
soaking in the monsoon of your fragile luxury.

I have written this poem into eternity,
for your children's children to meet with the truth.
But you have failed to read between these lines.
You have forgotten much too early for your kind.

So, I am saving this last ounce of brewing courage
To drink from the cup of justice and save myself from you.
To save this body and her country —a reincarnation.

To live here. To die here.
To be, here, home.

Fences
Pebofatso Mokoena

Sounds Like Home

(A tribute to Moses Molelekwa and Tembisa)

Angela Mthembu

Pen and ink
failed combat plans
drawn by conductors.
Desolating military tactics
that campaigned for attention signs
and united fists.
So, a piano man's praying hands
that were evenly placed
with fingers slightly bent
danced for Africa.
Wrists and palms placed
in the same class.
Piano hands all over this revolution.
Smothering minority rule.
His offering collected *spirits of Tembisa*
raised in Ecaleni section.
He mixed harmonies
that moved along Xubene routes.
Arranging major scales
Down rocky streets of Emfihlweni.
Trebling the *Bo Molelekwa* clan
stationed in Sedibeng
where his melodies rest.
Producing hymns
that sharpened *Biko's dreams*
of Ebony and Ivory strips
made in Difateng woods
planted in Emkhathini
where the *mountain shades* Moriteng.
His rhythmic patterns
moved whole notes up
Mqantsa hill,
over Ethafeni's Cliffs.
Strumming four fours

under Isiziba's tide
that attracted the moon to waves
and let the darkness
pass through
the gates of Esangweni
He swung *melancholy thoughts*
away from Emmangweni's grounds
that played the struggle
on and between the beat.
In the middle of Phumulong's acoustics
were *Ntatamoholo's genes and spirits*
transferred by Entshonalanga's
light
A piano man notated hope
into our home's name.
A piano man's hands
transcribed my home's story...

met die sterre gepla

Keith Lewis

american movies sê maak 'n wens as jy 'n skietende ster sien
snags wanneer die kattekoor hulle pers gesangboekies uithaal
en honde slapeloosheid begin smous,
kyk ek op na die charcoal nag plafon versier met konfetti
en ek voel weer dertien jaar oud op ons voorstoep
wagtend op 'n skietende ster om 'n wens te maak
en my pa is nog hier
hy fluister sy asem in my satellite skottels
'n skietende ster is die trane van sterre wat rou oor die sterfte van 'n chief
en 'n ster het geskiet. en die koeël het gedwaal. en 'n ster het geskiet.
en my pa is geskiet
die charcoal nag plafon versier met sparkling konfetti
lek

starstruck (met die sterre gcpla)

Tr. Pieter Odendaal

american movies teach us to make a wish when we see a shooting star
at night when the cat choir take out their purple hymn books
and the dogs start hawking insomnia,
I look up at the charcoal night ceiling decorated with confetti
and I am thirteen years old again on our front stoep
waiting on a shooting star to make a wish
and my dad is still here
he whispers his breath in my satellite dishes
shooting stars are the tears of stars mourning the death of a chief
and a star shot. and the bullet strayed. and a star shot.
and my dad was shot
the charcoal night ceiling decorated with confetti
leaks

Taste of freedom

Masoodah Mohamed

The old man shuffles along the line of weary bodies.
He lives two hours away from the city.
Today he will meet the doctor.

The old man clutches his hospital card
and green ID pass, patiently, for four hours.
He is smiling now – he has arrived at his turn.

The old man outstretches his palms,
left under right, his identity clearly in sight.
In the cradle of his autumn brown hands
wrinkles collect like gathered leaves.
Sharp, crisp, soft
is the old man's voice.
Goeie môre,
the old man bows.

Dumela Ntate Teboho! the young doctor smiles.
She doesn't call him Joseph,
the way those who don't look like him do.

Joseph Teboho Moloi is printed in black.
A boy on the farm, he learnt to sow seeds
for his daily bread. He swallowed his being -
divided his tongue in two.

He planted trees on oppressed soil
for so long, he memorised the sound
of water sinking into crops.
A migrant parched
he returned home
once every ninety days.

Years of servitude,
he uncurls his neck
hesitant to any form of respect.
Black holes expose captured tales
floating on creamy irises.

Dumela Mme! the old man rustles.

Ntate Teboho parts his lips some more.
He speaks of his pain like it doesn't ache.
The air makes way for his words.
The walls salute the sound of his ancestors.
His breath finds the home of its mother's arms.
Displaced from the womb,
the child returns.

Ezazalelwa Emqubeni

Mazwi Shazi

Ezazalelwa emqubeni
Azikwazi ukuqonda kungani sinamakhaza ezifubeni
Sigcine amaphakade aphela esthubeni
Asikwazi ukuwangcwaba ngoba kunalezi zingxenye zethu ezingaya
    nawo ethuneni

Ngakho kunganithusi uma siya empumelelweni singenamdlandla
Impi yendlala thina esqeda amandla
Kithi lonke igxathu eliyakhona ekuzakheni ukuhamba phezu
    kwamalahle
Siyimlingo yamathambo abambe izidumbu kahle kahle
Asilahlanga thawula empilweni
As'banga namandla okulithenga kwayisekuqaleni
Futhi Sekunezikhathi sijikisa izintambo emqaleni
Sithi sfuna uk'buyela kulobuya buthongo baphakade esasinabo
    ekuqaleni

Singcole sinjena nje uma siwa asisasiboni nes'dingo sokuba sizithintithe
NoMose wasifaka ebugqileni bokulwa nempilo mhla siphuma egibhithe
Kwezethu izimpilo zonke iziqephu
Bezingezandla zesikhathi zisishiya neziqhephu
Thina silwazi njengentende yesandla ukhwantalala
Sisenzulwini okanye ezulwini
Angazi kodwa ng'zama ukuthi kade saphangalala
Sawela kuleslwane senhlupheko mhla sthatha impilo ngamawala
Uyabona kithi impilo ngathi uhambo olubheke ethuneni
Imbangela ilendathane esithe sisakhula yaphangalala

Ngoba azigcinanga ngokusiphuca es'bathandayo izandla zesikhathi
Zibathwalisa inhlabathi ngezifuba
Yaqhubeka impilo ohambweni yasikhuba
Besinesineke nemihuzuko esiy'thole sfunda ukuthi isvinini siyabulala
Kodwa eqinisweni kumele ukhe ngejubane ubheke ekuzakheni
Ikakhulukazi uma ungabazi ubude bethuba

Nina nje ngoba nathola umusa seningasehlulela
Nathi sinibuke zitatanyiswa zempilo nizidlulela
Nishoda ngokuqonda
Nalembhalo ningangayithanda kodwa iwuqweqwe zingane zakwethu
lana sxebula izilonda

Ziyabhibha uma sizivalele
Nina qhubekani nemibuzo
Sesyothikazisa ngayo sisalinde uZwelo luslethele imshanguzo

Kodwa ukushlulela ningalokothi
Iskakhulu umanivungula ngothi esidla ngalo imbuya
Kulula ukwahlulela uma wazalwa impilo yakufumbathisa indathane
yezizathu zokuvuya
Aslinyazwanga inhlupheko kphela
Yasishaya impilo thina slinde amadoda ahambe ebuya
Kepha abasala basfundisa ukbekezelela zange sbalahle
Ukuthi sasingeke sizimile izinyembezi
Ngoba izolo basithathele izinqumo
Sebeyakhala namhlanje ngoba thina siyahluleka ukuziphatha kahle

Sesilinde isphetho thina lana endleleni
Singenavalo lokuya esihogweni
Siyolicisha lelo ngabi ngalezinyembezi esizikhalile ekuphileni
Uma nithi izulu yikhaya labangcwele
Bayingcosana abayowubona umbuso walo
Ngoba bangcolile abantu bazifihle ngamavesi benjalo

Singcono thina asibanga nezizathu zokukholwa ubukhona balo
Ngoba usizi esazalwa nalo
Belubokusigqamisela ibanga elihanjwayo
nobuhlungu esibuzwayo impilo uma ithi isvezela ubuhle bayo
Lombhalo awuzuba neningi labawuthandayo
Ngoba kuliqiniso
Awukwazi ukuba nokuqonda okugcwele
Uma wazalwa nengcebo igcwele izandla uze ufinye ngendololwane
Hhhayi nje ngathi esazalwa nezandla ezingezamaketango
Kepha mekumele sidwebe isthombe sempilo
Kanti futhi sfundile nokuthi

Ithemba elabo bonke abangakaliboni inamuhla ngengesphetho
Sopha saxakwa ukugula kwanganqamuka ngisho sesiwuthintile
   umphetho
Wake wathi omunye UNkulunkulu unathi njalonjalo
Sabe sesibuka ubuhlwempu bethu inzondo yakhe yakheka kanjalo
Uhleli nje estulweni sobukhosi akasisukumeli sifa isibhaxu sempilo

Ngiyazi ungacabanga ngimthela ngechilo
Noma angsamukeli ngokugcwele isipho sempilo
Ukuthi angazi ngzosamukela kanjani ngoba ngathi umangisivula
   ngabona akukho lutho
Ngakhula, ezigabeni zonke zobuhlungu ngadlula
Sengilindile nje ukuthi igcwale nakumina esfubeni
Ukuze mangfika kuye ngimnxuse phambi kokuya esihogweni
Ukuthi bonke abeza emuva kwami
Nabo kubafanele ukuzalelwa emqubeni.

Descendants of Privilege (Ezazalelwa Emqubeni)

Tr. Sabelo Soko

Descendants of privilege will never understand why we are cold inside
We are harbouring fleeting eternities that we cannot bury
To bury them is to send parts of ourselves to the grave too
Now, do not be startled when you see us trudging forward feebly
It is the war against poverty that consumes our spirits
Our building steps land on burning coals
We are magic bones holding this flesh, to be exact
We did not give up on life
We had nothing to give from the start
Noosed ropes have touched our necks
With the hope they can take us to that eternal sleep
That once held us before we woke up
To this moment

We are murky
We do not see the worth of purging ourselves when we fall
Moses left us enslaved by life after freeing us from our Egypt
All the episodes of our lives are about the hands of time
Hands that hand us lumps at the end
We know depression like palms, like the sand
We are 6 feet deep or maybe we are in the sky
I am not sure
What I am saying is that, we died a while ago
While chasing illusions of this life
We fell into a monstrous den called poverty
Our lives are now just a journey to the grave
Called upon by the myriads we buried when we were still young

The hands of time did not just take our loved ones
And cover their bones with sand
They also crippled our journey to the end
We grew patient with scars from the lessons that speed kills
How fast should one go when they build themselves
Unaware of the time they have

Yet you, descendants of privilege, still judge
We watch you from our noble homes living large
Lacking understanding
You may even dislike these words
They are scabs of wounds that will not heal when concealed
Now go on, blurt your questions
We will distract ourselves with finding the answers
While we wait for our healing
But dare not judge us
When your toothpick is the spoon that feeds us
It is easy to judge
When life has bundled you with reasons for joy
But as for us
It is not just the hands of time that left us in the den
It is also the longing for fathers who left a promise to return
We did not leave the ones we were abandoned with
We just could not stand their tears
The ones who taught us patience
Yesterday they took decisions for us
Today they weep because we cannot keep them too well

We are patiently waiting for the end of this path
Fearless of going to hell
For we have wept enough tears to extinguish its fires of sin
It is said that heaven is only for the holy
Then surely it will be entered by a few
For many are evil,
Hiding behind verses of the bible

Better we, who have never believed its existence from the beginning
For the grief we were born into
Is the summit of the painful journey that life takes us on to show its
    beauty

These words will not please multitudes
For this simple fact
It is hard to grasp the truth if you were born with a hand holding a
    silver spoon to your mouth

Unlike us, born with shackled hands and still expected to paint life's
    bigger picture well
We have learnt that tomorrow is for those who have not yet seen today
    as *the end*
We have bled, sickness has overwhelmed us
Even after we touched the hem of faith
God is always around us, some tell us
Yet when we look around, only resentment grows
For he must truly loathe us
To watch us being battered by the hands of time from his throne

Not showing gratitude for the gift of life
This might be blasphemous, I know
Yet what happens when the gift unwrapped reveals nothing
I am grown now
I know the exact extent of sadness
I am waiting for my load of sand to welcome me back
So I can go to heaven before heading to hell
To look God straight in the face and tell him
We all are worthy of privilege and grace.

Die Palimpses

Wade Smit

Hoekom sit jy in hierdie plek?
Hoekom sit ek ook?
Is dit nie die palimpses nie?
Wat in die nag wil skryf en krap
En wat die verlede in sy mond
Sal vat?
Die palimpses
Voorvader wat verbode is
Bringer van duidelikheid en mis
Pasop vir hom
En sy wrede hande twee
Voor hom en onder sy vlytige vingers
Sal selfs jou skoene en jou hare
Val soos dooie dinge
Soos blare en gras
Wat die papier sal wees
Van waar was jy gegooi?
En waar het jy beland?
Jy is die palimpses
Wat die riviere drink
En die verlede gryp
Soos 'n berg se goud
Wat in 'n ander land sit

The Palimpsest (Die Palimpses)

Tr. Pieter Odendaal

Why are you stuck here?
Why am I also stuck?
Is it not the palimpsest
That wants to write and scribble at night,
That will take the past in its mouth?
The palimpsest
Forbidden forefather
Harbinger of clarity and mist
Watch out for him
And his cruel two hands
In front of him and under his fervent fingers
Even your shoes and hair
Will fall like dead things
Like leaves and grass
That will be the paper
Where were you thrown from?
And where did you end up?
You are the palimpsest
Drinking the rivers
And grabbing the past
Like a mountain of gold
Stuck in some other country

you are here

Sarah Lubala

a. in the days after you left, the emptiness became our government. we owned a single mattress. we belonged to the floor. to the blunt charity of sleep.

b. in the Guardian, there is an article on tshiluba.

the journalist writes: "the failure of the language to be taught at school has resulted in the replacement of native words by French words". i want to say something about losing your way. about speaking to your mother and stumbling over your own name.

c. it's not the will to die. only to kill the thing. that girl in her school dress. eye of water. fist of quiet violets. the wick split with blue light. i must wait her out.

i go to lay down and there is a knife in the bed.

d. i like the word ghosting as active verb. how it turns loss to remembrance and remembrance to inheritance. how the smoke of a life goes up forever and ever.

e. in cape town, a friend points to a car guard, tells me 'they're all congolese'. i am a country wrung out. i am every person consumed out of their place.

Wherever your blood has dropped,
Will bossom a flower of exceeding sweetness,
Whose scent will be carried on by the wings of the air
And all the nations will inhale it.

tr. Robert Sobukwe

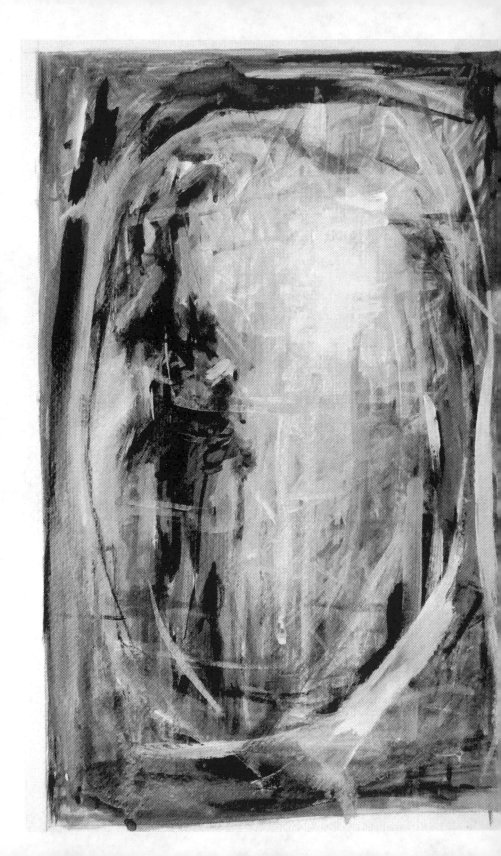

Battlefield
Mxolisi Dolla Sapeta

A Face of Many

Mthabisi Sithole

some people can only be imagined
breathing, unfurling
resting & busy
a being wonderful quietly taking to action,
some people can only be imagined
a being inhabiting a body
soft, the horror of hard eyes

when they smile, it is not only
between their lips, in teeth
it's also behind them
that smile fills them
spreads like rains, grips you
sits on their face and pulls
a day from the depths, dragging back
the sheets

some people can only be imagined
in their night,
at time's bank of leering anxieties
in cries and hushing
you were not there, to imagine
tomorrow, to imagine truly
not then but here,
here you are

I Know a Woman

Jennifer Sheokarah

I know a woman from fifty-six,
who took a monumental stand in politics.
I know her through my history book
that speaks of the prodigious battle.
Her name was honoured in ninety-five
and, even today, it's still alive.
I celebrate those women –
their mighty display of peaceful unity
allow women of today ample opportunity.

I know a woman from next door,
who took a beating to the floor.
I know her; she was on the front page:
it spoke of her abusive husband's wrath.
I wondered if he'd ever read a history book…
Could history save her from his grappling hook?
I pity that poor woman.
Our ancestors are turning in their graves,
watching some women being treated like slaves!

I know a woman from where I work,
who is a Deputy Principal with a powerful smirk.
I know her through her dominant voice
that defends her single-life decision.
She is old enough to be my mother,
but carries the 'Miss' like no other!
She is untouched by society's expectations,
Through this, our history proudly survives –
women are so much more than submissive wives.

I know a woman from the street corner
who sells brooms at night; would someone please warn her?
I know she's a single mother, making a living.
Towards the absent father, I'm entirely unforgiving.

She needs to work only in the day
before she becomes the brutal night's prey;
some men are cruel.
The fight to protect women goes on for centuries,
while the innocent battle with ghastly memories.

I know a woman, and that is me,
who wants what my mum could never be.
I know myself through conversations in the mirror
that speak of the achievements I want to bring closer.
I write my own cheques and drive my own car;
to empowered women, this won't sound bizarre.
I love both a man and my profession;
For this, I am grateful for the history –
it makes me soar above the mystery.

I know a woman, and that is you,
who needs to engage in all you can do.
I know a man that might hurt you;
we need to fight him if we want to blossom.
I know a woman who might dare;
I know a man who will show his care.
I know a woman who will fight to survive.
I know a man who will keep you alive.
Women: to yourself, be true.
Women: to YOURSELF, be true.

God: A black woman

Ntsako Mlambo

In the land of Kwa Nongoma
Women ruled the world
God was a black woman
And this realm ran on the roots of a matriarch

When God decided to speak things to light
She moulded the Heavens and Earth
With all the tenderness in Her hands
God commanded that all mortals
Who live on the terrains of Kwa Nongoma
Should ooze femininity just like Her
And this, this is how women were created

God was so in love with being a woman
That She came to the final decree
Of making women the Creators of Life
The Mothers of all Soul and Fertility
Women were God's disciples

Mkabayi was the King of all tribes
She was gentle on her people's cries
Never fed them lies
She could predict famines and drought
And would advise Modjadji and her children
To make it rain
Modjadji would gather uNomvula, Mvula, Mapula, Rrapula, Kunaya,
    Ojo, Hujan, Imvura and Mmiri Ozuzo
And they would dance into the night
Until the heavens cried

Nomsa The Mother of Compassion
Made babies from soil

Because the soil borrows us life
And the soil is what we will return to
When death claims us as Her own

Sara Baartman would rest
On the bellies of mountains and recite mantras
She would preach about consent
Told women that if anybody is to touch them
It must be someone they love
Someone they would want to touch as well
Sara told women to love their bodies for what they are

Krotoa The Mother of all Languages
Spent most days speaking in tongues
She would watch the way water moves
And listen to the waves play hymns
That usher dreams to sleep

All this came to an end
When Adam arrived from a telestial universe
Adam was quick to anger
And jealousy
He questioned why God
Was Black and Woman

So he stabbed God's heart
Drank Her blood
Erased Her history
And proclaimed himself the Creator of the human race
This is how patriarchy started

On the highways of human history
God's blood never stopped running
On the highways of human history
The blood of a black woman has been spilling

We see it in how our fathers beat our mothers
Dispose our bodies in ditches
Under bridges, in our backyards
In dust bins

Adam and his descendants
Keep on stabbing at our hearts

The world continues to burn

Another one of us will be killed
Today
And the God inside us all
Will continue to bleed

Carving a Goddess (out of your mother)

After Lawrence Lemaoana's "Democracy is Dialogue"

Xabiso Vili

In the garden of Eden,
your mother did not pick the apple
but plucked a Molotov cocktail
from her womb
and drank deep
until she was tipsy enough to seduce the serpent.

You come from a lineage of women
who went to war with children on their backs,
breastfeeding strangers' newborns in the trenches -
their spines gnarled and bent
on survival -
and pruning bruises into orchards.

Screaming into the night,
you have tossed boozy bottles at passing gods,
but ain't no miracle for a drunkard.

You know the underbelly of this city too well,
have flirted with its shadows,
misplaced hope in darkness,
put away childish things.

Still, songs of revolution put you to sleep,
violent lullabies
stolen from the first days.

Your back turns into a trunk,
chest hollowed out —
this is where you hoard your treasure.
You only bear fermented fruit,
roots as deep as longing.

This city feeds you
and from you.
You watch your mother
turn herself into a burning statue.

You drink her torch and start anew.

loving like our mothers

Busisiwe Mahlangu

i can sit here but i am running out of time
                    losing time is the first act of disappearance
you can kiss me while your nose bleeds into my mouth
                    your blood is not death. not a body begging for
                                        a funeral.
it is my father's burial in the next
house. the elders are asking for me
for my body to make tea and scones
                    show me other ways of grieving that are not just
                                        for you
the church women told me touching
a boy is a sin. letting a boy touch you
is a greater sin.
                    there is a hell colouring the ground open for us
my mother was seventeen when
she met him. a year older than me. two
years later my brother cleansed the sin
                    i need your comfort. only when i am ruined
i have a wound in my bones older
than me. it is my mother, locking
herself under my rib. safe and in love.
                    no, i cannot tell them i have a boyfriend.
i am losing time/disappearing/bleeding,
eating graveyard sand
opening the ground for   forgiveness
                    looking for a better man
                    a man who won't die with his mouth silent.

Incwadi Yokufa

Bongeka Nkosi

Mama, ngibhala lena zehla phoko,
Lan' amazw' okugcina, sengimagang' endlela,
Imishiz' isingidind' okhakhayini ngadela,
Cha ayidl' izishishiyele mtanomuntu, sekungenele,
Sengilibuke langenel' igceke leliba, lingifanele.
Mama, ekukhuleni kwami bengiyintombi ziphelele,
Ngiqhamuka kucokam' izimbali zingikhwahlele,
Ngiqhamuk' emikhawulweni kucwayiz' izikhitha zithule,
Nanamuhla kububul' umhlabath' ungiqhwel' elibeni!

Mama, ngisalizw' iphimbo lakho,
Liqhumis' isililo owawusikhihla kwaze kwasa nkwe,
Kwaze kwalamul' indonsa kus' isicim' emkhathini,
Kwaze kwaphum' ilanga selicwayiz' ezintabeni,
Kwabe sekuwukufulathel' egcekeni, ngibhek' emendweni,
Wangiyala ngelokugcin' elanginqind' inhliziyo, yathithiza
Uth' angibohloniph' umyeni ngithambel' isidwaba,'
Lalibethel' ihubo lesigcawu, lingivusel' amadlingozi,
Sekuyikh' ukududuz' inhliziyo ngitshiloze, ngingemlozi,
Indlel' isibangise kwamfaz' ongemama, kwelosizi,
Selimathunz' ezintaba nginikela kwaMkhathali,
Ngihuba ngingahubi - ngibubula ngibalisa ngenhliziyo!

Isidwaba sangishuka ngishundula, ngaqhum' ukhalo,
Nhlanhla leyo ngabeletha nami ngavundis' igceke,
Nab' oVusikhaya noVus'umuzi, bagcwel' igceke,
Kodwa sekwaxhakathis' izagil' ezingidinde kwasa,
Injabulo nemfudumalo beyethembisa kusaqala,
Yize mina nomyeni besinokungaboni ngaso linye,
Kepha nakh' ukuxabana kwethu kwajika,
Kwaphenduka intsakavukel' umchilo wesidwaba!

Sizothini lokh' ilumbo livela esidwabeni,
Nakhu phela esithubeni umyeni, waphenduk' indlavini,
Kwaqhum' imbedumehlwan' akwabe kusafana,

Waphenduk' ihata waklukla ezikaFaro izinkamba,
Waxozoma nsuk' evulel' isibhaxu senkalivasi,
Sekungubumaye-maye nsuku zatshwala, bheka!
Namaduk' izichib' aphenduk' amayakayaka!

Uyise wabantwana waxegelwa nayisimilo,
Ngehla ngenyuka ngimthungatha phansi-phezulu,
Nasemijuxuzwen' ezidwabeni zabany' abafazi,
Kade kwas' engidinda nsuku zatshwala,
Bengopha ngize ngophe amahluli, mama,
Cha ungehlul' umendo lokh' awuthunyelwa,
Ngingeke nguthwal' imithwalo ngibuye-ke,
Ngingaba yindab' egudwin' omakhelwane,
Bengangicokoful' bangeth' izic' umabuy' emendweni!

Mama, lihub' ihubo lomendo weliba lami,
Ungiphonsel' emthangaleni woKhokho nami,
Usuyosal' ungibhekel' abantwa bami,
Ngiloba le zehla phoko, lokh' sengiyaluthabath' uhambo.

A Letter of Death (Incwadi Yokufa)

Tr. Kwazi Ndlangisa

Mother, I wrote this while wailing,
These are my last words, as I am about to embark on a journey,
I have been hit over my head far too long,
I ask for your forgiveness, you – someone's child, I have had enough,
I can foresee the site for my grave... a great fit.
Mother, growing up I was a mountain of a girl,
When I walked, flowers rose in my honour,
When I walked on ends, everyone blinked in silence,
Even when the soil cries, dig me up from the grave!

Mother, I can still hear the echoes of your voice
Making me burst into tears like how you wept until dawn
Until the morning star crawled through the light of the horizon
Until the sun came through edges of the mountains,
That was when I gave my back to my home, on my way to my marriage.
Your advices have now got my heart torn,
You said I should respect my husband and stay humbled,
The songs were sung, songs that uplifted my spirit,
I can only console my heart by singing,
On my way to the world of women who are not mothers, the place
    filled with pain,
The light is now crawling behind the mountains, while on my way to
    the lands of fatigue
Singing yet not singing - my heart wailing!

The isidwaba weighed my back dawn,
Luckily I also gave birth and made home a warmest place,
Vusikhaya and Vus'umuzi are now all over our home,
But now I am held back by the pain I have endured throughout the
    night,
How promising the happiness and warmth were in the beginning,
Even though at times my husband and I could not see eye to eye,
Even when our fights turned
Into our daily bread!

What were we going to do because it all began when I got married,
In just a blink of an eye my husband turned into an angry fire,
That burnt an eye open, yet there was no way of looking back,
He turned into a hole that swallowed everything alcoholic,
Everyday he was filled with anger, boiling and ready to hit
Everyday slowly became chaotic, look!
Even the scarf on my head could no longer sit as a crown!

The father of my children went on and found greener pastures
  somewhere,
I went up and down searching for him
Even under other women's skirts,
He beat me throughout the day,
I bleed and even bleed blood clots, mother...
I have had my fare share in the marriage,
I can not even pack my bags and see my way back home,
I would become the talk of town,
They would give me names, "the one who could not stay in her
  marriage!"

Mother, sing the song of my marriage to my grave,
Throw me to the lands of my ancestors,
Look after my children
I wrote this while weeping, I am now embarking on a journey.

Wolf Girl

Kylin Lötter

When they pulled at my hair
And knocked in my teeth
They took the time to ask,
What are you? What are you? What are you?
With your blood so red
And your eyes so dead
With your bruises so blue,
What are you? What are you? What are you?
And I said through the tears
That made my eyes glint like angel-thrown spears,
I'm a girl. I'm a girl. I'm a girl.
When I tore at their flesh with my fangs and my claws
They looked at me and cried,
What are you? What are you? What are you?
And I answered with a smile, a smirk and a snarl,
I'm a wolf. I'm a wolf. I'm a wolf.
When I walked down the street,
Heel, toe, toe, feet.
They looked at me and pleaded,
What are you? What are you? What the hell are you?
I am Wolf Girl
And to me, you're just meat.

Mobile Homes
Pebofatso Mokoena

The keys of uMkhulu, Nduduzo Makhathini

(to the Jazz Abahlekazi(kazi), oGogo, noMkhulu)

Thandolwethu Gulwa

the waves of still, shivering
oceans

beautiful, tidy, tides,
neat,
a need for
that healing

At Your Feet, oh Lord!

bare, to the earth
that opens its
mouths

in half notes and crescendos
harmonies of a somehow
Con Spirito, not quite

more like *intlombe,*
sigida sikhanda
iinkambi

a wave of energy,
a wave of sound

Dimensions,
Heights
Reached

Notre Dame

Annathea Oppler

Somewhere,
      A cathedral is burning.
Eight hundred years of history
    falls over Paris,
  the yellow smoke
Our Lady's last lament.
    Ashes to ashes,
       to dust.

Continents away,
      You hold me tight.
We talk not of soaring ceilings,
  But of whitewashed walls,
      browned by the dusty Karoo,
  of
   art,
     Spiderman,
 Icarus,
and I try not to kiss you.

Somewhere,
    history goes up in flames
Here,
  fanned by the flames in our bellies,
  we are making a history
     of our own.

Somewhere,
  flames engulf the symbol
    of a people,
Here,
  flames are building a life.

~ 15 April 2019, Notre Dame burns

monolith

Tshifhiwa Itai Ratshiungo

it's a working world. a city a
lake across a village tapering
into the sun. we make it
across to get the value of our
sweat in a jungle of stone.
fancy living extracted from
the sprouts of our sacred
land. a chair, a couch, a cup of
coffee. our documented lives
to remind them of the place
from where we all began. to
watch a people living in a
land scarred towards barren.
success is scaling water with
our feet. to live a dream.
home is not a ruin. it's a
world working.

Cloaked with Words

Claire Mary Taylor

The witch comes at 3.05am
She's on fire
Burning on the pyre
You can hear nothing but her screams
She's come to warn you in your dreams
She knows about your magic
Knows your task is to mask it
She's seen your seeing
Hide it in the plain sight of madness
Everyone will mourn you with just a pinch of sadness
She knows there's no way out of this way of being
A gift made worse
by reality's readiness to ruin the mystical
Take your pills never be hysterical
Burn the old women's ways down
I've heard stories of her huts still being destroyed by men's false fears
Why is this still how we live?
forgetting the sanctity of healing hands
held out to free.

When words fail

Olivia Botha

Blue,
How will you go?
How will you face your end?

Ever fading
Flesh and bone
Ever blue,

How will you go?

Watching, waiting,
As flesh turns to bone
The slow passing of time
A lingering soul

Where will you go?
I wonder
Did you live the life you've always dreamt of?

Will you reach your nirvana?
Will you meet your Messiah?
As you fade from blue to white
What knowledge did you hold?
But never spoke

When words fail, and bones break
Where will we go?

As the sky turns from black to blue,
A dress from blue to white
And a mother becomes the messenger of another

A body draped in blue
An ever-fading
Blue to white

And I wonder,
did you ever speak in tongues?
En was dit 'n dubbele tong?

Untitled 2
Keneilwe Mokoena

About the judges

vangile gantsho is a poet, healer and co-founder of **impepho press**. Unapologetically black woman, she has travelled the continent and the globe participating in literary events and festivals. gantsho is the author of two poetry collections: *Undressing in front of the window* (2015) and *red cotton* (2018). She holds an MA from the University Currently Known as Rhodes (2016) and was named one of Mail & Guardian's Top Young 200 South Africans of 2018.

Her latest collection, *red cotton*, an exploration of what it means to be black, queer, and woman in modern-day South Africa, was named City Press Top Poetry Read of 2018, and long-listed for the National Institute for the Humanities and Social Sciences 2020 Award.

Tshifhiwa Given Mukwevho is an editor, proof-reader and writer. He is an award-winning bilingual author who writes in English and Tshivenḓa. His love for literature has had him read and recite his prose and poetry at several book festivals, schools, prisons, refugee camps and airports in South Africa, China, Algeria, Hong Kong and Dubai.

He participated in the Jozi Book Fair in SA (2011), Beijing International Book Fair in China (2014), Time of the Writer in SA (2015), FiSAHARA Festival in Algeria (2015 and 2016), Polokwane Literary Fair (2012 and 2015), and Vhembe Poetry Festival in SA (2015).

His published books include – among others – *A Traumatic Revenge* (short stories, 2011), *Mveledzo na Zwigevhenga* (children's book, 2015), *It Gets Deeper* (Poetry, 2020), *It Was Getting Late* (Poetry, 2017), *The Other Side of Darkness* (due 2020), *Nwananga Nandi!* (Drama, 2016), *Melody of the Soul* (Poetry, 2020). In 2020, he published a series of teen and young adult novellas, entitled *Kidnapped, A Sense of Respect, A Change of Heart, Bad Company*, and *Big Happiness*.

He heads Vhakololo Press, a publishing initiative which seeks to create a culture of reading and writing.

Nakanjani G. Sibiya was born in Eshowe, KwaZulu-Natal. He has authored several volumes of short stories, novels, dramas and co-authored or edited numerous anthologies of short stories and poetry. He has won awards for almost all his literary works; including the prestigious M-Net Book Prize for his debut novel, *Kuxolelwa Abanjani?* (2003). He recently translated *Kasikho Ndawo Bakithi* (a novel by MJ Mngadi) into English. His debut anthology of short stories in English will be released soon. Sibiya holds a Phd in isiZulu and is a lecturer at the University of KwaZulu-Natal.

Toni Giselle Stuart is a South African poet, performer and spoken word educator. Her work is widely published in anthologies, journals and non-fiction books locally and abroad. Her work includes *Krotoa-Eva's Suite – a cape jazz poem in three movements* – a poetry collection that re-imagines the story of Krotoa-Eva through her own voice; an excerpt of the work was adapted into an audio-visual piece, in collaboration with filmmaker Kurt Orderson (Amsterdam and Cape Town, 2016); Poetry, Paramedics and Film with filmmaker/health researcher Leanne Brady (2018); I Come To My Body As A Question with dotdotdot dance (UK & Sweden, 2016 - 2020); and What the Water Remembers at Woordfees (2020); forgetting. and memory with vangile gantsho & Vusumzi Ngxande, at the Virtual National Arts Festival (South Africa, 2020).

She is a Mail & Guardian Top 200 Young South African of 2013, and has an MA Writer/Teacher (Distinction) from Goldsmiths, University of London, where she was a 2014/2015 Chevening Scholar. She was the founding curator of Poetica, at Open Book Festival.

Contributors

Poets

Zizipho Bam is a South African poet, visual artist, and travel enthusiast born in East London. This 24-year-old award-winning poet creates work that seeks to heal self from mental illness, love, loss, and physical trauma. Navigating through the world as a young black womxn, Bam aims to investigate self and reveal how we relate with one another and the world. Using the body and its experience as inspiration, she reimagines pain to rewrite her experiences into a work of art.

Olivia Botha is an interdisciplinary artist with a focus on language. Her concepts revolve around how we communicate, or more so, how we are unable to communicate. Botha graduated from Michaelis School of Fine Art early 2017 with Dean's Merits List and is currently a resident artist at the Bag Factory in Johannesburg, South Africa. In 2018, Botha held a solo exhibition at SMAC Gallery after receiving the Cassirer Welz Award. Her films have screened at the National Gallery of Zimbabwe, the Labia in Cape Town, the International Short Film Festival in Italy and at Moderna galerija in Slovenia, amongst others. Botha is currently a nominee for the 2021 Berliner Künstlerprogramm and will attend a residency in France at SCAC Marestaing at the end of 2021.

Anathi Jonase was born in 1997 in Secunda in Mpumalanga, and moved to Idutywa in Eastern Cape in December 2008. At school he used to write motivational quotes which led him to write poems in his mother tongue isiXhosa. He completed his matric in 2016 and is now trying to study further. He was encouraged by a friend to write poems. This is his first work of art to be published.

Thandolwethu Gulwa kaNdungwana was born and raised in Phelandaba, Bloemfontein. She echoes the drumbeat of her ancestors through written word as a multilingual fiction and nonfiction writer, essayist, published poet and photojournalist. Gulwa is a Rhodes University Humanities graduate. She holds a Bachelor of Journalism and Media Studies degree, with specialisation in writing and Editing, and a B1 German Studies qualification. Her debut essay "A better life for all?" was published by Paperight in the *Young Writers' Anthology* (2013), and has opened her horizon to more published pieces by the Jip, Die Beeld, Die Volksblad, Bloemnuus, Bloemfonteinse Skrywersvereniging (BSV), Grocott's Mail and The City Press. Her name is engraved into awards such as the "Nie-moedertaal prys" awarded by the BSV.

Keith Oliver Lewis was born in 1994 in South Africa. In 2018 Keith's 17-year-old cousin, Nolan Davids, was murdered on school grounds by rival gang members. While writing Nolan's eulogy, Keith developed a love affair with words. In 2008 he attended New Orleans Secondary for their art program. This was also the year that the Lewis family moved to Smartie Town, a community with high gang related crime. Despite this, Keith excelled in the school newspaper and debating committee. He was chosen as head boy in 2012. He later traded his turquoise uniform for the maroon spring of Stellenbosch University to obtain a bachelor's degree in commerce, but pulled a Kanye West.

Nqobile Lombo is a professional architect residing in Johannesburg. Her interests are in spatial politics and architecture. She is also podcaster on Kwam, a space that navigates the socio-political issues that young black women experience in South Africa.

Kylin Lötter was born in Johannesburg, South Africa. She has been writing from a young age and enjoys the reality-breaking genres of Fantasy and Magical Realism as well as the feminist writings of Angela Carter and Virginia Woolf. She is currently a student at the University of Witwatersrand where she studies Philosophy and English Literature. Her poetry has appeared in Black Letter Media's Poetry Potion.

Sarah Lubala is a Congolese-born South African writer. She has been shortlisted for the Gerald Kraak Award and The Brittle Paper Poetry Award and long-listed for the Sol Plaatje EU Poetry Award. Her work has been published in Brittle Paper, The Missing Slate, Apogee Journal, The Shallow Ends, Entropy, and elsewhere.

Busisiwe Mahlangu, born 1996, is a writer, performer and TEDx Speaker from Mamelodi, Pretoria. Her debut collection *Surviving Loss* has been adapted and produced for theatre at the South African State Theatre as part of the Incubator programme 2018/2019. Mahlangu has toured and shared her work internationally including Washington DC, Sweden, Lesotho, Mozambique and Nigeria. Busisiwe currently runs her business Busi Creates where she makes jewelry and beadwork.

Ntseka Masoabi is a student studying towards a Master of Science in Geology, at Rhodes University. As a science student, he is also deeply fascinated and interested in the field of the arts, especially literature and portraiture. His aspirations and hopes are to be part of the United Nations Refugee Agency and Amnesty International, as a volunteer. He is also a physically active person who enjoys playing tennis and long-distance running.

Ntsako Mlambo is a writer from Daveyton, Benoni. She was raised speaking Zulu but her blood is of Tsonga origin. Mlambo is a quiet girl with loud dreams and spends most of her days dreaming. She believes that God is a black womxn and she will only come to save us if violence against women and children stops. Ntsako considers writing her superpower.

Masoodah Mohamed is a South African woman, a lover of art and a survivor of tragedy who weaves her emotions into metaphors and euphemisms.

Angela Mthembu or Angelyric is an expressionist who finds comfort in the medium of written and spoken word. Through evocative poetry she creates protest art that speaks against the imbalances created by systematic prejudices. Awarded the bronze prize in a Carfax writing competition, she has performed on stages in places such as Joburg and Soweto, Grahamstown Art Festival, Fete De La Musique and Smoking Dragon New Year's Eve Festival. She has done virtual performances for Giving poetry wings, Pick-me-up Poetry, Poetic Thursday's and is currently preparing to open at a heritage celebration presented by Nike South Africa.

Ronewa Mukwevho was born and raised at Muswodi Dipeni where he started his schooling at Malinge Primary School and went to Ratshibvumo Secondary afterwards. Mukwebo loves to write poetry, short stories and drama. He is eager to publish his book one day.

Masindi Netshakhuma was born in 1996 Itsani village outside Thohoyandou, Limpopo. She is currently furthering her studies with the University of Limpopo (Turfloop campus). As a great tributary payer of tradition and culture, Netshakhuma found it necessary to enrol at a cultural school named Indoni in 2017. She released her first English poetry book titled *Vision & legacy* in 2018, and her second book in 2020.

In 2019, her poem titled "Lushie" became one of the winning poems in the Avbob Poetry Competition. She is one of the English students among other international youth at Kelas Daring this year (2020).

Bongeka Nkosi is a young lady at the age of 18 from a small town called Estcourt. She is currently doing grade 10 at Abantungwa High School. She was brought up being taught that *"Knowing where you come from will definitely lead you where you want to go"*. She writes in isiZulu with the intention of promoting her mother tongue. She uses poetry as her therapy to face current social issues. One day she sees herself as a published and performing poet who uses her poems to heal, bring hope and inspire the nation.

Cebolenkosi Thalente Nkosi is a 22 year-old fourth-year student studying Bachelor of Education degree at the University of KwaZulu Natal. He grew up in a small village called Magaga, which is under Nqutu town. Nkosi was raised by his Aunt after his parents passed away. As a young poet, he makes use of social media to share his poetry and performances. Sthembiso Ntanzi played a very essential role in photographing and editing his work. Nkosi hopes to grow his skills in writing and poetry.

Annathea Oppler was born in Johannesburg and grew up on a farm in the mountains of North West province. She draws her inspiration from life encounters, family, nature, current events, and more recently, love in her poetry. Oppler is a Psychology graduate student at UCT, she hopes to go into the field of psychology to try make a difference in South African communities through critical engagement and empowerment. As an aspiring poet, this is her first work to be published.

Tshifhiwa Itai Ratshiungo is a writer and creative studying law at the University of the Free State. Most recently, a selection of his poetry was published on African Writer. He is available on Instagram and Twitter @_tshifhiwa

Mazwi Shazi is a poet from Durban who started writing in 2013. He has gone on to share his work in many South African poetry stages including Sundowners Poetry and Jazz, Poetry Africa Prelude poet in 2018, DFL Lover plus another, Hear My Voice Poetry Relief, and CSP Provincial slam to mention a few. He is a writer who would love to see his work grow and shared in more spaces and platforms.

Jennifer Sheokarah was born in 1993 in the South Coast of KwaZulu-Natal. She holds a Bachelor of Education (summa cum laude), an Honours degree in Language and Media Studies (summa cum laude), Masters in Education (cum laude) and is enrolled for a PhD in Education, all from the University of Kwa-Zulu Natal. Jennifer has served as tutor, demonstrator, marker and contract lecturer in various modules, and has been actively involved in community service projects while working for the Department of Student Residence Affairs at the campus. She has been awarded numerous scholarships, including a PhD Research Exchange scholarship to Norway and a Doctoral scholarship. Presently, Jennifer is an English educator in Richards Bay. Her hobbies include photography and writing.

Mthabisi Sithole is a Johannesburg-based poet. His poetry often addresses the collecting of past and present personal/private narratives alongside the world at large. His poetry is published in *Ja. Magazine*, *Teesta Review: A Journal of Poetry and Best New African Poets* 2019 anthology.

Wade Smit is a queer writer born in oThongathi, KwaZulu-Natal. He is currently pursuing his Master's degree in Historical Studies at the University of Cape Town under the History Access programme, where his research focuses on the conceptual history of *"umbuso"* in isiZulu literature. Wade currently writes and edits for the Amandla! Liberation Heritage Route, and the Durban Local History Museum's blogs in isiZulu and English. He founded the publishing project Kwasukela Books which, before its closure in 2020, published two books of isiZulu speculative fiction.

Claire Mary Taylor was born in Marondera, Zimbabwe in the winter of 1990. She was schooled in Swaziland as well as in many other provinces in South Africa including the North West, Eastern Cape and KwaZulu-Natal. Having spent her twenties living all over South Africa including several years in Johannesburg and Cape Town as well as numerous years spent living abroad in Ireland and travelling Europe, she has been described as an African gypsy. She now resides in Durban. She draws inspiration from these varied experiences of movement and transformation to write poetry that aims to capture the personal as well as the collective cultural experience. She is the author of two collections of yet to be published poetry called *Memories of Forgetting* and *Learning*

How to Study History which touch on themes of mental health, gender issues and personal as well as our joint histories.

Mbasa Tsetsana is an actor, writer and director. He has two published plays with Off The Wall Plays. His most prominent production, *Waiting for Nelson*, premiered at the South African State Theatre in 2014, as part of the Youth Expression's Festival. When he isn't putting pen to paper, Tsetsana acts on stage and on screen, having landed roles in the award winning and Academy Award nominated film, *Knuckle City* (2019), written and directed by internationally acclaimed director, Jahmil X.T Qubeka. Tsetsana has also written for Bomb Productions, where the writing team won a South African Film and Television Award for best achievement in scriptwriting. His passion for people and quintessentially cathartic South African stories are what drive his writing, acting and directing.

Xabiso Vili is a performer, writer and social activist. He is the champion of multiple slams and poet of the year for 2014 and 2015. Xabiso has been published in various anthologies. He has performed all over Africa, Europe, the U.S. and India. He strongly believes that art influences his community positively and is constantly working towards creating alternative stages for art to be shared. Xabiso also runs writing and performance workshops and has assisted in producing other award-winning writers and performers. He released his album, *Eating My Skin*, created with Favela Ninjas in 2016. His one-man show *Black Boi Be* has travelled extensively to critical acclaim in 2017 and *Laughing in My Father's Voice,* his debut collection of poems was released in 2018. In 2019, he was awarded the Digital Lab Africa Web Creation Prize and has spent 2020 creating a digital art exhibition called "Re/Member Your Descendants".

Translators

Domina Napoleon Munzhelele is a family man, history teacher and radio producer from Bileni village in Musina. He has produced 65 dramas including 1285 episodes of the soap opera *I khou khidzhana*. He has also written twelve radio dramas that have been broadcast on Radio Venda/ Phalaphala-FM since 1993 and has ten literary awards under his belt. Munzhele has written 25 books, some of which have been prescribed by the Department of Education, University of South Africa, University of Venda and Tshwane University of Technology. He is currently a writer for the Phalaphala-FM soapie, *Ndi yone mini yeneyi* and produces a soapy called *Ndi tshiwo* funded by National Arts Council. Munzhele has also worked as a journalist, a translator, project manager, publisher, reviewer and editor. He is the CEO of Development of Limpopo Literature and the Managing-Director of World Tongues Publishers, Masisi Publishers and Limpopo Faces.

Kwazi Ndlangisa is a multi award-winning poet from South Africa; published writer and translator based in Durban but rooted in the rural areas of UMzimkhulu, Chamto in KwaZulu-Natal. His writings are a golden thread through Africanism and spirituality and are inspired by his surroundings and his inner being. He believes that writing and reading poetry is a perfect channel to collect self back to its true purpose in both the psychological and spiritual realm. Ndlangisa is the Managing Director and Co-founder of Pot of Art (a house for creative arts). He has been published in a number of poetry anthologies and magazines across the country and is the author of *Collecting Self*, a poetry chapbook.

Mbongeni Nomkonwana is an entrepreneurial Innovative trailblazer with more than ten years of professional experience in traditional theatre, applied theatre, industrial theatre, and spoken word performing and touring Southern Africa. He is adept at translating isiXhosa literary texts into English and vice versa, and versed in acting, puppetry, comedy, and activations. Nomkonwana is co-founder, director of, and resident poet at Lingua Franca Spoken Word Movement: one of Cape Town's premier poetry collectives, with a unique fusion of spoken word poetry and authentically South African music. He has served as a panelist and performer at the annual Open Book Festival Poetica Programme and has featured at festivals such as Joburg Arts Alive, Franschhoek

Literary Festival, and Woordfees. In April 2018 Lingua Franca was invited by Northwestern University and Poetry Foundation for a two weeks residency, to deliver talks (on Lingua Franca's pedagogies) and performances at the university and around the city of Chicago. His published work can be found on: *ConVerse* by InZync Poetry as contributor, translator, and editor.

Pieter Odendaal is a poet, performer, translator and editor. His debut collection, *asof geen berge ooit hier gewoon het nie* (Tafelberg), was awarded the 2019 Ingrid Jonker Prize. He is the director of InZync Poetry and co-editor of the translation anthologies *Many Tongues* (2013) and *ConVerse* (2018). He is completing his PhD in socially and ecologically engaged spoken word poetry at the Queensland University of Technology in Brisbane.

Sabelo Soko is a Johannesburg based writer and performer from eMkhondo, Mpumalanga. With over 16 years multimedia experience, Soko's catalogue includes projects in film, advertising, studio records and stage productions. He is passionate about original stories and the preservation thereof.

Illustrators

Banele Khoza is a Swaziland-born, South Africa-based visual artist. He enrolled at the London International School of Fashion in Johannesburg, but soon realised that his passion was drawing. Khoza holds a BTech in Fine Arts from Tshwane University of Technology, Pretoria. In 2017 he won the prestigious Gerard Sekoto Award and with it a three-month residency at the Cité Internationale des Arts in Paris. His solo exhibitions include *Temporary Feelings* at the Pretoria Art Museum (2016), *Lonely Nights* at Lizamore Gallery (2017), and *LOVE?* at Smith Studio in Cape Town (2018). Khoza also headlined the solo exhibition titled *LGBTQI+:* Banele Khoza was part of the Curatorial Lab at Zeitz MOCAA (2018), opened BKhz (2018) and was recognized as one of the Mail and Guardian Young South Africans 2019 for the work they do at BKhz.

Keneilwe Mokoena is a visual artist, curator and educator based in Johannesburg. She is a Fine Art graduate from Tshwane University of Technology. Mokoena's work varies between multidisciplinary visual arts; art curation, direction and facilitation. Her work has been exhibited across South Africa and internationally including Swaziland, Brussels and Paris. Mokoena is the recipient of the Reinhold Cassirer award for 2015. She has curated several exhibitions in the Southern African region (including Maputo and Harare) for Capital Arts Revolution [an artist's collective from Pretoria], and Social Life of Waste [S.L.O.W] Art - a network of artists, researchers, writers, gardeners and community developers working within the discourse of waste. She forms part of the Talent Unlocked Artist Programme facilitated by Visual Arts Network of South Africa (VANSA) and Assemblage. She is currently one of the directors of The Project Space Organization since 2019.

Pebofatso Mokoena, born 1993 in East Rand, South Africa. He completed his NDip (Visual Art) at the University of Johannesburg and, apart from working towards his Bachelor of Arts, Pebofatso is a sessional tutor in drawing and presentation at the Faculty of Art, Design and Architecture at UJ. Mokoena has held 3 (three) solo exhibitions - *The Pebofatso Experience at HZRD, Inside Jobs at the Bag Factory,* and *Internal Probes* at David Krut Projects. His curated exhibitions include *Diptych; Disclosure - SMAC; Fresh Produce, Songs of Sankofa* - First Floor Gallery Harare, *Inner Nature, Fortunes Remixed - Bag Factory and South African*

Voices: A New Generation of Printmakers - Washington DC. Mokoena's work lies in public and private collections such as: *The Dimension Data* collection London; the Springs Art Library Collection, the Africa First collection, the South African Embassy Art Collection in Washington, D.C. and the JP Morgan Global Collection amongst other private and public collections.

Mxolisi Dolla Sapeta was born in 1967 in New Brighton, Port Elizabeth and began showing his work in public in 1989. He taught art for six years from 2001 in the division of art and design in Port Elizabeth College. Subsequent to publishing his first collection of poems in 2019 he continues to pursue his art as a full-time painter and writer and is constantly collaborating with other artists. Sapeta initiates platforms that attempt to promote art education in the townships where he continues to live and give art classes to immediate communities. He has participated in numerous group exhibitions in South Africa (including eight solo exhibitions) and internationally.

Printed in the United States
by Baker & Taylor Publisher Services